Rose Elliot's Book of Breads

Rose Elliot is the author of several bestselling cookbooks, and is renowned for her practical and creative approach. She writes regularly for the *Vegetarian* and has contributed to national newspapers and magazines as well as broadcasting on radio and television. She is married and has three children.

D1353312

Other titles available in the series

Rose Elliot's Book of Fruits
Rose Elliot's Book of Salads
Rose Elliot's Book of Vegetables

Rose Elliot's Book of

Breads

Fontana Paperbacks

First published by Fontana Paperbacks 1983

Set in 10 on 11pt Linotron Plantin
Illustrations by Ken Lewis,
except page 3 by Vana Haggerty
Made and printed in Great Britain by
William Collins Sons & Co. Ltd, Glasgow

Introduction

Few things can compare with the inviting aroma of freshly baked bread filling the house and the satisfaction of serving bread which you have baked yourself. And, contrary to what many people believe, breadmaking is a straightforward process which can easily be mastered.

EQUIPMENT

Most of the equipment necessary for breadmaking is simple and basic and to be found in any kitchen. Accurate measuring equipment in the form of scales, a set of measuring spoons and a jug are essential. You will also need a pair of scissors, a fork and a round-bladed as well as a sharp knife. The mixing bowl must be big enough to hold 1.4 kg (3 lb) flour with space for mixing. You will need cling film to cover the bowl or a large polythene bag to enclose it while it is rising, a pastry brush if you want to glaze the bread and a cooling rack.

Although the process of kneading dough can be soothing and therapeutic, if you're planning to make bread regularly you might find it worthwhile investing in a food processor or mixer with dough hooks. These work well and certainly save time. Look for the strongest, most robust you can find.

Bread tins

When it comes to choosing tins, I think the best are the old-fashioned oblong tins with high slanting sides (page 7). These are available in 500 g (1 lb) and 900 g (2 lb) sizes. It's useful to have two of each size although two of the smaller size are fine to start with. The tins must be well greased before use and during storage to prevent them from rusting. Non-stick bread tins are now available and help to prevent sticking, although I find these still need careful greasing.

If you are making bread for the first time, or do not have bread tins, the bread can be shaped and baked on a baking sheet, or cake tins can be used.

INGREDIENTS

Flour

When you are breadmaking, the most important element in flour is the gluten. This is a mixture of proteins in the flour which absorbs water and forms elastic strands. These stretch to contain the air bubbles and form the walls of the holes. The elastic properties of the gluten are therefore most important for a good rise in breadmaking. The gluten holds the shape of the bread until the temperature in the oven sets it.

Some flours contain more gluten than others. These are called 'strong' flours; ones with less gluten are known as 'soft'. Strong flour

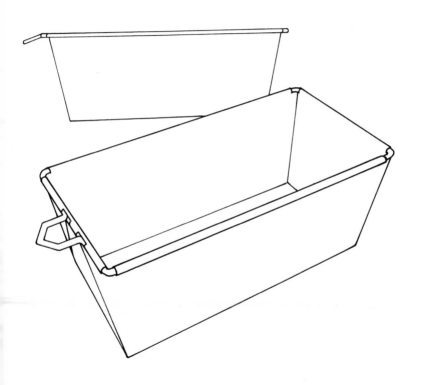

is the best for breadmaking, although I have made very successful wholewheat loaves using home-produced, soft, wholewheat flour.

As well as being strong or soft, flours are defined by the 'rate of extraction'. This means the percentage of the whole grain left in the flour after it has been milled. The name of the flour is a guide to the amount of whole grain it contains.

Wholemeal or wholewheat flours, as the name suggests, contain the whole of the cleaned wheat grain, nothing added or taken away. The presence of the bran and wheatgerm in wholewheat flour means that bread made from it is darker and heavier than that made from lower-extraction flours, but it has a rich, nutty flavour and is certainly the best from the health point of view as it is an excellent source of dietary fibre. Stoneground wholewheat flours are ones which are ground between stones instead of metal rollers. This keeps the grain at a lower temperature thus preserving more of the nutrients. These flours are usually more expensive and obtainable at health shops. As wholewheat flour contains the wheatgerm it can go rancid if stored too long, so buy from a shop with a brisk turnover and do not store for longer than two months.

Wheatmeal flours contain between 80-90 per cent of the original cleaned wheat grain. Merely by looking at the colour you can see that brown wheatmeal flours contain some of the bran and germ. As with wholewheat flour, buy in quantities that you know you can use up fairly quickly.

White flour usually contains around 70-72 per cent of the cleaned wheat grain. The milling process removes much of the bran and germ and this gives the flour its white colour. Flour becomes whiter and improves in quality if kept for several months. Normally the bleaching and ageing process is achieved chemically by adding various substances such as chloride dioxide, though unbleached flour can be bought at health shops. White flour, by law, also has to be fortified by certain nutrients to replace those removed during the milling process: thiamine, nicotinic acid and iron. Calcium is added as well.

Other flours such as barley and rye used to be the main bread flours before yeast was introduced as the raising ingredient. These flours are not extensively used now because of their low gluten content, though small quantities can be used to vary the colour and texture of the bread. You can also buy speciality bread flours, such as scofa and granary. These are made up by the miller and consist of wholewheat, wheatmeal or white flour with other ingredients such as wheatgerm, bran, malt, rye, barley or soya flour added.

I use wholewheat flour for most breadmaking, although I like to make different types of wholewheat bread for variety and I sometimes use wheatmeal and occasionally unbleached white flour or a mixture of white flour and wholewheat for a complete change.

Yeast

Yeast is the raising agent that makes the bread rise. It comes in two forms, fresh and dried, each with its loyal advocates. Baker's yeast should not be confused with brewer's or tonic yeast, neither of which is suitable for breadmaking.

Because yeast is a living plant, it needs food and the right conditions in order to work. As the yeast grows it gives off carbon dioxide and it is this gas within the dough that rises it. As the gas expands, the elastic cell walls of the gluten in the flour stretch to form the risen structure. The food that the yeast needs to do this job must be supplied as another ingredient in the bread recipe and the right condition is in the form of warmth.

Fresh yeast Also called compressed yeast, this is the easiest type of yeast to use and can usually be bought from health shops, bakers and some large supermarkets. It's usually sold by the 25-g (1-oz) weight and should be creamy beige in colour, moist, crumbly and sweet-smelling. A dark or mottled colour, a sticky or very dry texture, and an 'off' smell mean that the yeast is stale and will not work. Fresh yeast will keep for up to a week in a screw-top jar in the refrigerator.

Dried active baking yeast This is sold in packets and tins and looks like small beige pellets. It is available from most large supermarkets. Dried yeast is twice as concentrated as fresh yeast, so you only need half the quantity. It works just as well as fresh yeast once it has been reconstituted as described on page 14.

Dried yeast, like fresh yeast, should be fresh. Stored properly on a cool, dry shelf, dried yeast will keep in good condition for at least six months. If you do not bake your own bread regularly it is uneconomical to buy large quantities; buy the packets which are sold in 25 g (1 oz) and 50 g (2 oz) sizes. If using dried yeast from a drum or tin, make sure that, after you have removed some, there is no air space between the lid and the yeast: as you use the yeast fill the gap with some crumpled kitchen roll or cottonwool. If you do not do this the dried yeast will gradually lose some of its potency and its valuable rising qualities will be lost.

'Easy blend' This is a new variety of dried yeast which, unlike the conventional type, is mixed directly into the flour without having to be reconstituted. It looks like fine sand and is sold in packets of foil sachets. Each sachet contains 7 g (¼ oz) and is equivalent to 25 g (1 oz) fresh yeast or 15 g (½ oz) conventional dried yeast. You simply add this yeast to the flour before mixing in the liquid.

The amount of yeast needed depends on the richness of the dough, the rising time and temperature, and the method of mixing. The more fat and sugar a dough contains, the more yeast it needs to raise it; a dough given a long, slow rise requires less yeast than one which is quickly risen. Using too much yeast produces a crumbly, sour-tasting bread which stales quickly, although 'easy blend' yeast is an exception to this rule.

Liquids

The liquids used may be milk, water or a mixture of the two, or sometimes, for special results, a fruit or vegetable purée, as in the recipe on page 53. When all milk or a proportion of milk is used, the dough is strengthened. Milk improves the food value and texture of the bread and will, to a certain extent, delay staling.

The amount of liquid needed varies according to the type of flour being used, but a guide is to use a scant 250 ml (½ pint) liquid to each 450 g (1 lb) flour. Liquids are generally added lukewarm: this starts the yeast working immediately.

Salt

Salt brings out the flavour of the bread and, to a certain extent, controls the action of the yeast. It is essential that the amount is carefully measured because too much will inhibit the raising action of the yeast, while too little will give a sticky, unmanageable dough.

Fat

The addition of fat improves the texture and volume of the bread and helps to delay staling. Fat has a softening action on the gluten in flour and this improves the elasticity of the gluten, resulting in an increased rise. Margarine, butter, a hard white fat or vegetable oil are all suitable.

Other ingredients

Eggs can be mixed into the flour in place of some of the liquid to enrich and soften the dough, resulting in a more cake-like consistency; dried or crystallized fruits, nuts, extra sugar and spices can also be added, as can savoury ingredients such as chopped onion, herbs and grated cheese. A basic bread dough can also be rolled out and topped with sweet or savoury mixtures, as in pizzas; or it can be spread with butter, rolled, folded, chilled and then used to make flaky croissants or Danish pastries.

HOW TO MAKE A LOAF OF BREAD

For one 900 g (2 lb) loaf or two 450 g (1 lb) loaves

15 g (½ oz) fresh yeast; *or* 2 teaspoons dried yeast plus ½ teaspoon sugar; *or* 1 packet easy-blend yeast
400 ml (¾ pint) warm water
700 g (1½ lb) strong plain flour: wholewheat, wheatmeal, white or a mixture
2 teaspoons salt
15 g (½ oz) butter

1. *Preparing the yeast*
Put 150 ml (¼ pint) of the warm water (taken from the quantity

required for the recipe) into a small bowl or jug. Fresh yeast works best at about 25°C (78°F); this is suitable for dried yeast too, although that is activated more quickly at a higher temperature – 40°C (104°F), but no higher than this or you will kill it. You don't have to measure the temperature exactly; the water should feel pleasantly warm.

If you're using fresh yeast, crumble this into the liquid and stir to blend the yeast with the water.

For dried yeast, first stir half a teaspoonful of sugar into the water then sprinkle the yeast on top, stir and leave in a draught-free place for 10-15 minutes until the yeast has frothed up like a glass of beer. (If it fails to froth up it means that the yeast is not working: either the yeast has been stored for too long or the water was too hot and you will have to start again with a new batch.)

Easy blend yeast is added with the flour: see next stage.

2. *Preparing the flour*
Weigh the flour and put it with the salt and fat in a large bowl. Rub the fat into the flour with your fingertips, as if you were making pastry, until it is all incorporated and there are no lumps. If you're using 'easy blend' yeast, sprinkle this in now.

3. *Adding the yeast liquid*
Make a well in the centre of the rubbed-in mixture and pour in all the yeast mixture and the remaining water. Mix by drawing the dry ingredients into the liquid with a wooden spoon. Mix together until

the dough begins to bind together and leaves the sides of the bowl to form one mass; flours vary in the amount of water they can absorb and sometimes it may be necessary to add a little more liquid or a small quantity of extra flour in order to achieve this.

Sometimes in a recipe for an enriched dough containing eggs and fat, the yeast is added by a different method, called the sponge batter method. In this case the yeast is mixed into a batter with a third of the total amount of flour given in the recipe, plus the entire quantity of liquid (which must be at blood heat) and at least one teaspoonful of sugar. No salt is added at this stage. This batter is left for about 20-30 minutes until it froths up like a sponge. The remaining ingredients are then added: see page 56.

4. *Kneading*
The dough is kneaded next to ensure a good rise and texture to the bread. When the yeast is added to the flour it has the effect of softening the gluten. Kneading offsets this softening effect and makes the dough strong enough to hold in the gas bubbles which the yeast produces and to hold the firm structure of the dough. Kneading stretches and thereby strengthens the gluten. It interlocks the gluten strands, helping to form a firm structure to hold up the bread until it is set by baking.

Kneading is a simple process of stretching and pushing the dough. Do this either by hand or with the dough hook of an electric mixer, until the dough feels firm and elastic. It is a satisfying process to feel the dough change as you knead it; it starts off as a sticky, lumpy mass and gradually becomes smooth, supple and silky.

Kneading by hand Place the dough on a lightly floured surface and very lightly flour your hands. Keeping your fingers together, fold the dough towards you. Then push down and away with the heels of both hands stretching out the dough. Now fold it back towards you again, so that it is compact. Give the dough a quarter turn so that it will be stretched in a different direction. Repeat the process. You should develop a rocking action as you knead and turn. Continue to knead for 10 minutes.

Kneading with a dough hook If you are using a mixer with a special dough hook attachment, kneading time can be reduced considerably. Prepare the yeast liquid in the mixer bowl, add the rubbed-in flour mixture directly to the liquid in the mixer bowl. Mix the dough using the slowest speed for 1 minute before increasing the speed to moderate for a further 5 minutes.

5. *Rising*

When the dough has been thoroughly kneaded, put it into a large, lightly oiled bowl and cover the bowl with cling film or oiled polythene, or stand the bowl inside a polythene carrier bag, to create a moist atmosphere, and keep in the warmth. Leave the dough until it has doubled in bulk and springs back when pressed lightly with a floured finger.

For a speedy rise, put the dough in a warm draught-free place. A

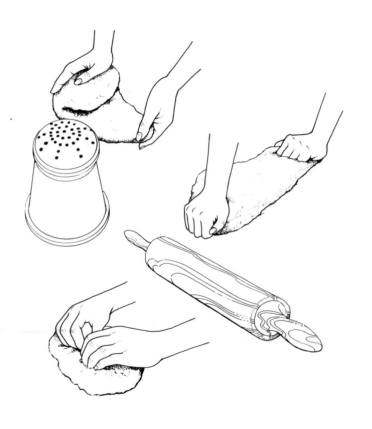

warm linen cupboard is ideal, or a cupboard next to or near hot water pipes. Do not stand it on top of a radiator if there is considerable bottom heat.

By choosing your temperature for rising (see chart) you can control the rising time. In a warm atmosphere the dough will rise in an hour or less. If you're out all day you may find it more convenient to leave the dough to rise in a cold place or even in the refrigerator overnight or while you are away.

First Rising Times

In a warm place 23°C (74°F)   45-60 minutes
   e.g., an airing cupboard, by pilot
   light on gas cooker

At room temperature 18-21°C   1½-2 hours
   (65-70°F)

In a cool room or larder   8-12 hours

In a refrigerator   up to 24 hours
   (brush dough with oil and cover bowl
   with greased polythene to prevent hard
   crust forming)

6. *Knocking back*

During rising the dough may develop large, unevenly spaced holes. To remove these the risen dough is 'knocked down' or 'knocked back'. Punch it with your hand to make it collapse, then put it on a clean working surface and flatten it firmly all over with your knuckles. Knead the dough again quickly until it is firm and elastic.

This is the time when other ingredients such as dried fruit and sugar can be added; simply put them on top of the dough and gradually work them in as you knead the dough. These are not usually added earlier because the weight of the dried fruit can slow down the rising of the dough and extra sugar can inhibit the action of the yeast. After this final kneading the dough is ready for shaping or putting into tins for its final rise and bake.

7. *Shaping bread dough*

A well-made bread dough that is smooth and elastic is a joy to handle and will lend itself to imaginative shaping if you have time to spare. All the shapes described below can be made with the quantity of dough given on page 13, and there are other ideas in the recipe section of the book.

For a tin loaf It is essential to choose the right size tin for this kind of loaf; the dough should fill two thirds of the tin so that there is room for rising. If the tin is too full the dough will rise and spill over the edges. For a small 450 g (1 lb) tin cut off a piece of dough weighing 500 g (1 lb

2 oz); for a larger 900 g (2 lb) tin use 1 kg (2 lb 4 oz) dough. To shape the dough for a tin, flatten it into a rectangle three times the width of the tin, then fold into three. Turn it over with the seam underneath and drop into the tin. Press the dough into each corner and down the sides with your fingers; this will make sure the bread fills the tin properly and will also give the bread a good rounded shape.

Cottage loaf Divide the dough in two, one piece twice as large as the other and shape into rounds. Place the larger of the two rounds on to a prepared baking sheet with the smaller round on top. Use the floured handle of a wooden spoon or a floured finger to join the two rounds together by pressing the handle or finger down through them until you almost reach the baking sheet. For a traditional touch, once the two rounds have been joined together, the sides can be notched by snipping with the tips of the kitchen scissors (see drawing, page 57).

Bloomer A bloomer loaf is a long loaf that is slashed five times across the top; when the dough rises for the second time it 'blooms' out. Shape the dough into a fat sausage about 30 cm (12 in) long and slash the top with a sharp knife.

Cobs and batons These are traditional shapes which are usually made with wholewheat, wheatmeal or granary dough. For cobs, shape the dough into a ball and place on a greased baking sheet. Flatten slightly with the palm of your hand, then using a sharp, lightly floured knife,

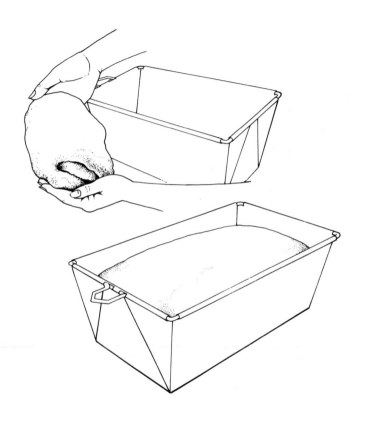

cut a deep cross in the top of the dough. For a baton, shape the dough into a sausage about 30 cm (12 in) long. Shape each end to a point, then slash the top diagonally in two parallel lines.

Plait Traditionally made from dough which has been mixed with milk instead of all or part of the water and enriched with extra butter (50 g/2 oz for 700 g/1½ lb flour), though an ordinary dough can be used. Divide the dough into three equal pieces, roll each into a sausage about 30 cm (12 in) long, fat in the middle and tapering at the ends. Start plaiting from the centre, finish the ends off to a neat point.

Round rolls Often made from a milk and butter dough as given on page 31, but ordinary dough can be used. Divide the dough into pieces weighing about 50 g (2 oz) each. For simple round rolls, put the piece of dough on the working surface and use your palm and a circular motion to roll it into a ball. Press down on the roll then ease your hand up to cup your fingers around the ball, still using a circular motion. Continue doing this until you have a perfect ball shape with a whirl mark underneath – this shows that the dough has been rolled correctly. Put the rolls on to a greased baking sheet. Allow about 4 cm (1½ in) between each one if you want crisp rolls. For soft rolls place them about 10 mm (½ in) apart so that when they rise for the second time they will join up.

Finger rolls Take 50 g (2 oz) of dough and flatten it with your hands.

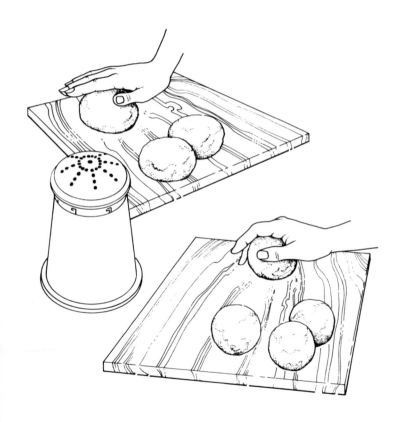

Using the palm of your hand roll the dough into a ball-shape then place the dough on to a lightly floured surface. Using the palm of your hand, roll the dough into a sausage shape, approximately 6.5 cm (2½ in) long.

Other roll shapes Baby cottage loaves, bloomers, plaits, cobs and batons can be made for a change. Use 50 g (2 oz) dough and follow the descriptions given for shaping the loaves, above. For clover leaf rolls divide the dough into three equal pieces, roll these into balls and place them close together on the baking sheet so that they will join up as the dough rises.

8. *Proving the dough*
Once the dough has been shaped and put into tins or on a baking sheet it is ready for its final rise, called 'proving' because it proves that the yeast is still working. The bread needs to be covered with polythene and left to rise as before. When covering the bread make sure you leave enough room for it to rise: it should double in size during this last rising. A polythene carrier bag, lightly greased and tied loosely round the tin or tins, is probably the most convenient covering at this stage.

The time taken for this final rising will again depend on the temperature, but will be less than for the first rising (see chart opposite).

Second Rising (Proving) Times

In a warm place 23°C (74°F) e.g., an airing cupboard, by pilot light on gas cooker	30 minutes
At room temperature 18-21°C (65-70°F)	40-50 minutes
In a cool room or larder	2-3 hours
In a refrigerator: brush surface of dough with oil and cover with greased polythene; leave at room temperature for 15 minutes before baking	up to 12 hours

9. *Glazing and decorating*
Once it has risen to double its size, the bread can be baked as it is, or it can be finished by being brushed and sprinkled with various ingredients to give a particularly attractive appearance. For a crusty loaf, brush with salted water (1 part salt to 3 parts water); if you want a shiny golden finish, use top of the milk or beaten egg, or melted butter or margarine for a crisp, crunchy crust. After being brushed with any of these the loaves or rolls can be sprinkled with kibbled wheat, poppy seeds, sesame seeds or other seeds such as caraway or cumin.

10. *Baking*

Bread needs to be put into the centre of a hot oven: 220°-230°C (425°-450°F), gas mark 7-8. This high temperature is necessary to kill the yeast quickly and prevent the dough from rising further. The gluten is set by the heat and becomes the framework of the bread. The temperature is usually reduced to 200°C (400°F), gas mark 6 after about 10 minutes: be guided by the individual recipe.

The bread is done when the crust is golden and the bread sounds hollow, like a drum, when it is taken out of the tin and tapped underneath with the knuckles. Remove the bread from the tin immediately it is cooked and transfer to a wire rack to cool.

Almond Plait

A flaky roll with a moist filling of almond paste.

MAKES ONE LARGE PASTRY

½ quantity of croissant dough
  (page 35)
225 g (8 oz) almond paste
2 tablespoons apricot jam, sieved
  and warmed

2 tablespoons flaked almonds
a little icing sugar

Make flaky dough exactly as described for croissants on page 35; roll
out to a rectangle about 35 cm x 25 cm (14 in x 10 in). Roll almond
paste into a strip 32 cm (13 in) long and 7.5 cm (3 in) wide and place
down the centre of the dough, so that there is about 7.5 cm (3 in) of
dough either side of it. Make diagonal cuts in these side pieces about 1
cm (½ in) apart as shown in the diagram on page 28, then fold
alternate strips over to make a plaited effect, tucking in the top and
bottom ends neatly. Place plait on a baking sheet, cover and leave to
rise for about 30 minutes, until puffy. Set oven to 220°C (425°F),
gas mark 7. Bake plait for 25-30 minutes. Brush with apricot jam,
sprinkle flaked almonds down centre. Cool on wire rack; sprinkle
with icing sugar.

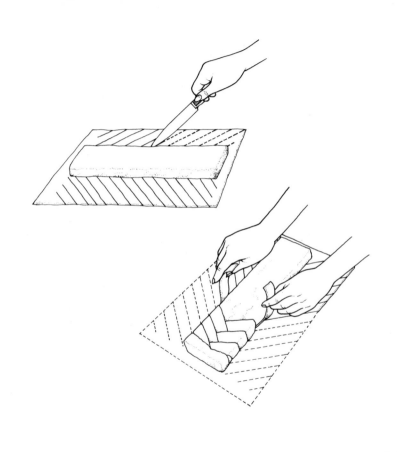

Easy Baps

Quick and easy to make using easy-blend yeast, these are delicious for breakfast or with a savoury filling.

MAKES 8

150 ml (5 fl oz) milk
150 ml (5 fl oz) water
50 g (2 oz) butter
225 g (8 oz) wholewheat flour
225 g (8 oz) strong white flour

1 teaspoon salt
1 teaspoon sugar
7 g (¼ oz) packet of easy-blend yeast

Heat milk, water and butter gently until butter melts; cool to lukewarm. Mix flours, salt, sugar and yeast in large bowl, add milk mixture and mix to a dough. Knead 5 minutes, put into a bowl, cover and leave in a warm place for about 1 hour, until doubled in bulk. Set oven to 220°C (425°F), gas mark 7. Knock back dough, knead briefly. Divide into 8 pieces, form into smooth rounds, dust with flour and place well apart on a floured baking tray. Cover and leave in a warm place for 15-20 minutes, until well-risen. Bake for 15-20 minutes. Cool on a wire rack.

Bran Bread

This extra high fibre bread tastes good and has a pleasantly light texture.

MAKES TWO 450 G (1 LB) LOAVES

15 g (½ oz) fresh yeast or
    2 teaspoons dried yeast and
    ½ teaspoon sugar
475 ml (17 fl oz) warm water
700 g (1½ lb) wholewheat flour

50 g (2 oz) bran
1 tablespoon sugar
2 teaspoons salt
1 tablespoon oil

Dissolve yeast in a cupful of the measured water; if using dried yeast add sugar too and leave for 10-15 minutes until frothed up. Mix flour, bran, sugar, salt and oil in a large bowl; add yeast liquid and remaining water and mix to a dough. Knead for 5-10 minutes, cover and leave until doubled in bulk: about 1 hour in a warm place. Knock back, knead lightly, shape and put into greased tins. Cover and leave until dough has doubled in size again: about 30 minutes. Set oven to 230°C (450°F), gas mark 8. Bake bread for 10 minutes, reduce heat to 200°C (400°F), gas mark 6 for a further 25 minutes, then turn on to a wire rack to cool.

Bread Rolls

It's easy to vary these rolls; roll them in flour and place them closer together (1 cm/½ in apart) for soft rolls you pull apart; brush with melted butter or beaten egg for a crisp crust. You can also replace the beaten egg in the mixture with a little extra milk if preferred.

MAKES 12

15 g (½ oz) fresh yeast or	350 g (12 oz) wholewheat flour
2 teaspoons dried yeast and	1 teaspoon salt
½ teaspoon sugar	25 g (1 oz) soft butter
150 ml (5 fl oz) lukewarm milk	1 egg, beaten

Blend yeast with milk; for dried yeast add sugar too and leave for 10-15 minutes to froth. Combine flour and salt in large bowl, rub in butter. Add yeast liquid and egg; mix to a dough. Knead 5-10 minutes. Put dough in bowl, cover and leave until doubled in bulk: 1 hour in a warm place. Knock back, knead lightly; then divide into 12 pieces and form into rounds. Place 2.5 cm (1 in) apart on greased baking sheet, cover and put in warm place for 30 minutes, until very puffy. Bake rolls at 220°C (425°F), gas mark 7 for 20 minutes. Cool on wire rack.

Brioches

These classic French rolls make a delicious breakfast treat.

MAKES 12

15 ml (½ oz) fresh yeast or
   2 teaspoons dried yeast plus
   ½ teaspoon sugar
2 tablespoons warm water
225 g (8 oz) strong plain flour

½ teaspoon salt
1 tablespoon sugar
50 g (2 oz) soft butter
3 eggs, beaten

Dissolve the fresh yeast in the warm water; if using dried yeast add the sugar too and leave for 10-15 minutes until frothy. Mix flour, salt and sugar; add yeast, butter and eggs to make a sticky dough. Knead dough for 5 minutes, adding a little more flour if necessary. Put dough into a bowl, cover and leave for 1-1½ hours until doubled. Punch down, divide into 12 pieces. Remove a quarter of each piece, roll rest into a ball, place in greased bun tin, make hole in centre with your finger. Roll remaining piece of dough into a small ball, place on top. Cover and leave to rise for 1 hour, until puffed up. Set oven to 230°C (450°F), gas mark 8. Bake brioches for 10 minutes, serve warm.

Cheddar and Walnut Bread

Serve this crisp-crusted, richly flavoured bread warm from the oven with home-made soup, pâté or cheese and salad.

MAKES 1 ROUND LOAF

15 g (½ oz) fresh yeast or
   2 teaspoons dried yeast and
   ½ teaspoon sugar
200 ml (7 fl oz) hand-hot water
275 (10 oz) wholewheat flour

1 teaspoon salt
15 g (½ oz) butter
75 g grated Cheddar cheese
50 g (2 oz) walnuts, chopped

Dissolve the yeast in the water: for dried yeast, add the sugar too and leave 10-15 minutes until frothy. Mix flour and salt in a bowl; rub in butter. Add yeast liquid and mix to a fairly soft dough. Knead 5-10 minutes, put dough into a bowl, cover and leave until doubled in size: 1 hour in a warm place. Knock back dough and knead in the cheese and nuts. Form into a round loaf, place on greased baking sheet. Cover and leave until well risen: 20-30 minutes. Bake loaf at 230°C (450°F), gas mark 8 for 10 minutes, then turn setting down to 200°C (400°F), gas mark 6 and bake for a further 15-20 minutes. Cool on a wire rack.

Christmas Fruit Loaf

MAKES ONE LARGE LOAF

15 g (½ oz) fresh yeast or
   2 teaspoons dried yeast and
   ½ teaspoon sugar
100 ml (3½ fl oz) lukewarm milk
450 g (1 lb) wheatmeal flour
pinch of salt
50 g (2 oz) brown sugar

125 g (4 oz) softened butter
½ teaspoon powdered cardamom
2 teaspoons vanilla essence
grated rind of 1 lemon
225 g (8 oz) mixed candied fruits
2 eggs, beaten

Mix yeast with milk; if using dried yeast, add sugar too and leave until frothy: 10-15 minutes. Mix flour, salt and sugar; rub in butter. Add yeast liquid and remaining ingredients. Mix to a soft dough, knead for 10 minutes. Cover and leave until doubled in bulk: 1 hour in a warm place. Punch down, form into a loaf shape, place in greased 900 g (2 lb) tin. Cover, leave in warm place for 30 minutes, till dough has reached top of tin. Set oven to 180°C (350°F), gas mark 4. Bake for 45 minutes. Cool.

Crumpets

Crumpets are fun to make and surprisingly quick and easy. If you haven't got crumpet rings you can use egg-poaching rings. I have also successfully used an 18-cm (7-in) flan ring, cutting the crumpet into quarters for serving!

MAKES ABOUT 12

15 g (½ oz) fresh yeast or
    2 teaspoons dried yeast and
    ½ teaspoon sugar
300 ml (11 fl oz) hand-hot milk
    and water mixed

225 g (8 oz) flour
1 teaspoon caster sugar
1 teaspoon salt
butter for greasing

Dissolve yeast in the milk and water; if using dried yeast add sugar too and leave for 10-15 minutes to froth. Combine flour, sugar and salt in a bowl; add yeast liquid, mix to a smooth batter. Cover and leave in a warm place for 45 minutes until frothy. Grease frying pan and crumpet rings with butter. Place rings in frying pan, set over a low heat. Half-fill rings with batter. Cook gently for about 5 minutes until tops are set and covered with little holes. Remove rings, turn crumpets over to cook top for 1-2 minutes. Serve immediately or cool then toast.

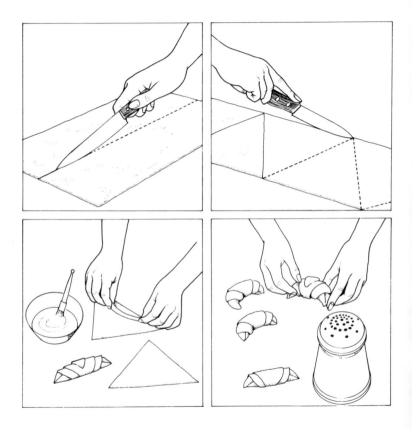

Croissants

MAKES 12

200 g (7 oz) butter	450 g (1 lb) strong plain flour
25 g (1 oz) fresh yeast	1 teaspoon sugar
250 ml (½ pint) warm water	beaten egg to glaze

Mix a bread dough as described on page 13 using 25 g (1 oz) of the butter and no salt; knead 5 minutes, then roll out to a long rectangle about 1 cm (½ in) thick. Dot one third of remaining butter over top two thirds of dough, leaving 1 cm (½ in) border. Fold bottom third of dough up over centre, then fold top third down. Turn dough so fold is on right-hand side; press edges with rolling pin to seal. Repeat rolling and folding twice, using rest of butter. Put dough in polythene bag in fridge for 1 hour, then roll into rectangle 54 cm x 35 cm (21 x 14 in) and cut in half lengthwise. Cut each strip into six triangles with a 15 cm (6 in) base (see diagram, page 36). Roll triangles up from base, brush with egg, curve into crescents, place on baking sheet. Prove for 30 minutes. Set oven to 220°C (425°F), gas mark 7. Bake croissants for 15-20 minutes.

Danish Pastries

MAKES 15

1 quantity of croissant dough
  (page 35)
50 g (2 oz) mixed dried fruit
40 g (1½ oz) caster sugar

1 teaspoon mixed spice
125 g (4 oz) marzipan
beaten egg to glaze, glacé icing,
  flaked almonds

Roll dough out ½ in (1 cm) thick and divide into three equal pieces.
Roll one of these into an oblong, 30 cm x 20 cm (12 x 8 in), sprinkle
with dried fruit, sugar and spice, roll up like a swiss roll. Cut into 6
pieces, make two deep cuts in each, open out slightly. Cut both
remaining pieces of dough into 6 and roll each into a square about 10 x
10 cm (4 in x 4 in). Cut marzipan into 12 pieces. Make six of these into
2.5 cm x 10 cm (1 in x 4 in) strips. Place a strip of marzipan at top edges
of 6 squares of dough, roll up, make cuts along length and curl round
to make cockscomb. Form rest of marzipan into rounds, place one in
centre of each remaining square of dough and fold corners to centre.
Brush all with beaten egg. Set oven to 220°C (425°F), gas mark 7.
Leave pastries for 20 minutes, until puffy, then bake for 20 minutes.
Cool, then ice and sprinkle with flaked almonds.

French Bread

25 g (1 oz) fresh yeast or
   15 g (½ oz) dried yeast and
   ½ teaspoon sugar
300 ml (10 fl oz) hand-hot water
700 g (1½ lb) strong, plain,
   unbleached, white flour

2 teaspoons salt
2 teaspoons sugar
25 g (1 oz) soft butter
yellow cornmeal or extra flour for
   coating

Dissolve the yeast in the water; if using dried yeast, add sugar too and leave for 10-15 minutes until frothy. Combine flour, salt and sugar in a large bowl; rub in butter. Add yeast liquid, mix to a dough, adding a little more liquid if necessary. Knead for 10 minutes, then put dough into a clean bowl, cover and leave until doubled in size: 1 hour in a warm place. Knock back, knead briefly, put dough back into the bowl and rise again: 40-45 minutes. Knock back, divide dough in two, sprinkle working surface with cornmeal, roll dough into two long thin baguettes. Place on greased baking sheet, cover and prove for 30 minutes. Brush with cold water, bake at 200°C (400°F), mark 6, for 1 hour, brushing crust with cold water every 10-15 minutes.

Yeasted Fruit Cake

This light, semi-sweet cake is easy to make and good with coffee.

MAKES ONE 20 CM (8 IN) CAKE

1 level tablespoon dried yeast	2 eggs
6 tablespoons lukewarm milk	125 g (4 oz) soft margarine
25 g (1 oz) sugar	grated rind of 1 orange
225 g (8 oz) flour	225 g (8 oz) mixed dried fruit
1 teaspoon salt	3 tablespoons demerara sugar

Put dried yeast, milk, sugar and 50 g (2 oz) of the flour into a bowl and mix. Cover, leave in a warm place until sponge-like: 30-40 minutes. Then add rest of ingredients, beat vigorously for 4-5 minutes. Pour into greased 20 cm (8 in) round tin. Cover, leave 30-40 minutes until doubled in size. Sprinkle with demerara sugar. Bake at 200°C (400°F), gas mark 6 for 30-35 minutes. Cool on wire rack.

Granary Cob

This crusty round loaf is delicious with butter and honey.

MAKES ONE 900 G (2 LB) LOAF

25 g (1 oz) fresh yeast or
   15 g (½ oz) dried yeast and
   ½ teaspoon sugar
400 ml (¾ pint) hand-hot water
700 g (1½ lb) granary flour

1 tablespoon sugar
1 tablespoon salt
25 g (1 oz) butter
kibbled wheat for topping

Dissolve yeast in a cupful of the measured water; if using dried yeast add ½ teaspoon sugar too and leave for 10-15 minutes until frothed up. Put flour, sugar and salt into a large bowl; rub in butter, then pour in yeast liquid and remaining water and mix to a dough. Knead for 5-10 minutes, put back in bowl, cover with polythene or cling film and leave until doubled in bulk: 1 hour in a warm place. Knock back, knead lightly, shape into a round. Sprinkle with kibbled wheat. Place on greased baking sheet, then cut a deep cross in the top. Cover and leave in a warm place for 30 minutes until well risen. Set oven to 200°C (425F), gas mark 7. Bake for 40-45 minutes. Cool on rack.

Grant Loaf

This is my adaptation of the bread invented by Doris Grant, pioneer of healthy eating. It's well flavoured and very quick to make because it only rises once and isn't kneaded.

MAKES 2 450 G (1 LB) LOAVES

15 g (½ oz) fresh yeast or
  2 teaspoons dried yeast and
  ½ teaspoon sugar
425 ml (15 fl oz) hand-hot water

500 g (1 lb 2 oz) wholewheat flour
1½ teaspoons salt
2 teaspoons sugar
kibbled wheat for topping

Dissolve yeast in a cupful of the water; for dried yeast add ½ teaspoon sugar too and leave 10-15 minutes. Combine flour, salt and sugar, add yeast liquid and water to make a sticky dough. Spoon into two greased 450 g (1 lb) tins – it should half-fill them. Sprinkle with kibbled wheat, cover, leave to rise to within 1 cm (½ in) of top of tins: 30 minutes at room temperature. Set oven to 200°C (400°F), gas mark 6. Bake bread for 30 minutes. Cool on wire rack. For 6 small loaves, use a 1.4 kg (3 lb 5 oz) bag of flour, 50 g (2 oz) yeast, 1.3 litre (2¼ pints) water, 2 level tablespoons sugar and a slightly rounded tablespoon of salt.

Herb Bread

This only takes 2 hours to make from start to finish.

MAKES ONE 450 G (1 LB) LOAF

6 tablespoons milk
6 tablespoons hot water
15 g (½ oz) fresh yeast or
   2 teaspoons dried yeast and
   ½ teaspoon sugar
275 g (10 oz) wholewheat flour
4 teaspoons sugar

1 teaspoon salt
25 g (1 oz) soft butter or
   margarine
1 small onion, peeled and grated
½ teaspoon each oregano and
   rosemary

Mix milk and water, blend in yeast. If using dried yeast add sugar too and leave for 10-15 minutes to froth. Combine flour, sugar and salt in large bowl, rub in butter or margarine, add onion and herbs. Pour in yeast and mix to a dough; knead for 5-10 minutes. Put dough back in mixing bowl, cover and leave until doubled: 45 minutes in a warm place. Set oven to 230°C (450°F), gas mark 8. Knock back dough, shape and place in greased 450 g (1 lb) loaf tin. Cover, leave 20-30 minutes to rise. Bake for 10 minutes, then reduce setting to 200°C (400°F), gas mark 6, for 25 minutes. Serve warm.

Hot Cross Buns

Fragrantly spiced buns, fun to make, and delicious served warm.

MAKES 12

1 quantity bread roll dough
(page 31) kneaded and
risen once
½ teaspoon each mixed spice,
cinnamon, grated nutmeg

75 g (3 oz) currants
40 g (1½ oz) chopped mixed peel
25 g (1 oz) sugar

For the crosses
75 g (3 oz) shortcrust pastry

For the glaze
2 tablespoons milk
25 g (1 oz) sugar

Knock back dough, add the spices, currants, peel and sugar and
knead dough until they're mixed in. Divide dough into 12 pieces,
form into rounds, place 2.5 cm (1 in) apart on greased baking sheet.
Cover and put in warm place for 30 minutes until well puffed up. Set
oven to 220° (425°F), gas mark 7. To make crosses, roll pastry thinly,
cut into strips and arrange in crosses on top of buns (or just cut
crosses). Bake for 20 minutes. Heat milk and sugar until sugar is
dissolved; brush over buns. Cool on rack.

Mixed Grain Bread

This bread has a delicious flavour and chewy texture.

MAKES ONE 450 G (1 LB) LOAF

15 g (½ oz) fresh yeast or
  2 teaspoons dried yeast and
  ½ teaspoon sugar
200 ml (7 fl oz) hand-hot water
175 g (6 oz) wholewheat flour

75 g (3 oz) rye flour
25 g (1 oz) kibbled wheat
75 g (3 oz) medium oatmeal
1 teaspoon salt
1 tablespoon oil

Dissolve the yeast in the water; if using dried yeast stir in the sugar too and leave in a warm place for 10-15 minutes until frothy. Combine the flours, wheat, oatmeal, salt and oil in a large bowl; add the yeast liquid and mix to a dough. Knead 10 minutes, place in bowl, cover and leave until doubled in bulk: 1 hour in a warm place. Knock back, knead briefly, shape and put into a greased 450 g (1 lb) loaf tin. Cover and leave in a warm place until doubled in size. Bake loaf at 220°C (425°F), gas mark 7, for 10 minutes then reduce to 200°C (400°F), gas mark 6, for a further 20 minutes. Cool on a wire rack.

Nut, Raisin
and Honey Bread

A slightly sweet bread that's delicious sliced and buttered for tea.

MAKES ONE 450 G (1 LB) LOAF

15 g (½ oz) fresh yeast or
  2 teaspoons dried yeast and
  ½ teaspoon sugar
150 ml (5 fl oz) warm water
225 g (8 oz) wholewheat flour

1 teaspoon salt
15 g (½ oz) butter
50 g (2 oz) each flaked almonds,
  raisins and honey

Dissolve the yeast in the water; for dried yeast add sugar too and leave 10-15 minutes until frothy. Mix flour and salt in a bowl, rub in butter. Mix to a dough with the yeast liquid, knead 5-10 minutes. Put dough in bowl, cover, leave until doubled in size: 1 hour in a warm place. Knock back, then knead in the almonds, raisins and honey. Shape and place in greased 450 g (1 lb) loaf tin. Cover and leave until centre of bread is 2.5 cm (1 in) above top of tin. Bake at 230°C (450°F), gas mark 8, for 10 minutes, then turn down to 200°C (400°F), gas mark 6, for a further 20-25 minutes. Turn out on to a wire rack to cool.

Pear Bread

Here a moist filling is rolled up in a light dough. It's delicious with coffee.

SERVES 6-8

1 quantity bread roll dough
    (page 31) risen once

For the filling

125 g (4 oz) stoned prunes, 225 g (8 oz) dried pears (from health shops) and 50 g (2 oz) seedless raisins, simmered in 275 ml (½ pint) water until thick

rind and juice of ½ lemon
ground cinnamon, grated nutmeg
1 tablespoon Kirsch
beaten egg to glaze

Knock back and briefly re-knead the dough, roll out to a 38 cm x 38 cm (15 in x 15 in) square not more than 6 mm (¼ in) thick. Add lemon, spices and Kirsch to dried fruit mixture. Spread dough with fruit filling, roll up firmly, prick all over, place on baking tray. Cover with cling film, put in warm place to prove for 30 minutes, until puffy. Set oven to 180°C (350°F), gas mark 4. Brush roll with beaten egg, bake for 35 minutes. Serve warm.

Pitta Bread

MAKES 12

15 g (½ oz) fresh yeast or	450 g (1 lb) wholewheat flour
2 teaspoons dried yeast plus	2 teaspoons salt
½ teaspoon sugar	1 teaspoon sugar
300 ml (½ pint) hand-hot water	1 tablespoon oil

Crumble fresh yeast into the water and mix until dissolved; or stir dried yeast and sugar into the water and leave for 10-15 minutes until frothed up. Combine flour, salt, sugar and oil in a large bowl; add yeast liquid, mix to a dough then knead for 5 minutes. Cover dough with cling film, leave until doubled in bulk: 1 hour in a warm place. Punch down dough, knead lightly. Set oven to 230°C (450°F), gas mark 8. Divide dough into 12 pieces, roll each into an oblong, 18 cm (7 in) long and 8 cm (3 in) wide. Place on oiled baking sheets, put in a warm place for about 15 minutes until puffy. Bake for 5 minutes, then reduce temperature to 200°C (400°F), gas mark 6 for 10 minutes. Cool on wire rack, then split pitta breads open by inserting a sharp knife in the top and sliding it along, separating the two layers.

Pizza with Cheese, Onions and Tomatoes

SERVES 4

15 g (½ oz) fresh yeast or
  2 teaspoons dried yeast plus
  ½ teaspoon sugar
150 ml (5 fl oz) warm water

225 g (8 oz) wholewheat flour
1 teaspoon salt
1 tablespoon oil

For the topping
2 tablespoons oil
1 large onion, peeled and
  chopped
1 clove garlic, crushed
1 350 g (12 oz) can tomatoes, very
  well drained

salt and freshly ground pepper
125 g (4 oz) cheese, thinly sliced
1 teaspoon oregano

Make dough for base as described for pitta bread, page 49, until dough has doubled in bulk at end of first rising. Fry onion in oil for 10 minutes, add garlic, tomatoes and seasoning; cool. Roll dough into a 30 cm (12 in) circle, place on oiled baking sheet, spread with tomato mixture, sprinkle with cheese and oregano. Set oven to 200°C (400°F), gas mark 6. Let pizza stand for 15 minutes, then bake for 20 minutes.

Potato Bread

The potato helps the action of the yeast and results in a particularly light, moist bread.

MAKES TWO 450 G (1 LB) LOAVES

15 g (½ oz) fresh yeast or
   2 teaspoons dried yeast and
   ½ teaspoon sugar
225 ml (8 fl oz) water
450 g (1 lb) strong flour:
   unbleached white or
   wholewheat

1 teaspoon salt
15 g (½ oz) butter
200-225 g (7-8 oz) cooked potato

Dissolve yeast in the water; if using dried yeast add sugar too and leave mixture 10-15 minutes until frothy. Mix flour and salt, rub in butter. Add yeast liquid and potato and mix to a dough. Knead 10 minutes, place in bowl, cover and leave until doubled: 1 hour in a warm place. Knock back, form into two loaves, put into greased 450 g (1 lb) tins. Cover and leave in warm place for 30 minutes until very well risen. Bake at 230°C (450°F), gas mark 8 for 10 minutes, then turn down to 200°C (400°F), gas mark 6 and bake for a further 20-25 minutes. Cool on a wire rack.

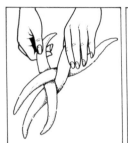

Poppy Seed Plait

25 g (1 oz) fresh yeast or
   15 g (½ oz) dried yeast plus
   ½ teaspoon sugar
400 ml (¾ pint) warm milk
700 g (1½ lb) strong plain flour

1½ teaspoons salt
1½ teaspoons sugar
50 g (2 oz) butter
beaten egg, to glaze
poppy seeds

Blend yeast into the milk; for dried yeast add sugar too and leave for 10-15 minutes until frothy. Put flour, salt and sugar into a large bowl, rub in butter. Add yeast liquid, mix to a dough. Knead for 10 minutes, put into a bowl, cover and leave until doubled in bulk: 1 hour in a warm place. Knock back, knead briefly, then make a plait as described on page 22. Put on greased baking sheet, cover and prove for 30 minutes, until puffy. Set oven to 230°C (450°F), gas mark 8. Brush plait with beaten egg, sprinkle with poppy seeds and bake for about 35 minutes. Cool on wire rack.

Quick Bread

You can reduce breadmaking time dramatically by adding ascorbic acid or vitamin C to the dough: this speeds up fermentation so that the bread can be ready in 1¾ hours.

MAKES ONE 900 G (2 LB) LOAF OR TWO 450 G (1 LB)

25 g (1 oz) fresh yeast	700 g (1½ lb) strong flour
400 ml (¾ pint) warm water	1 tablespoon salt
25 mg ascorbic acid tablet, crushed, from chemists	1 teaspoon sugar
	15 g (½ oz) butter or margarine

Dissolve yeast in the water, add ascorbic acid. Mix flour, salt and sugar, rub in the butter or margarine. Make a well in the middle, pour in yeast liquid, mix to form a dough. Knead for 5-10 minutes, then put dough in a bowl, cover and leave 5 minutes – dough will increase by one third. Knock back, knead briefly, shape and place in tins. Cover bread and put in a warm place until doubled in size: 40-45 minutes. Bake at 230°C (450°F), gas mark 8, for 30-35 minutes for small loaves, 40-45 minutes for large ones. Cool on a wire rack.

Rye Bread with Treacle and Cumin

MAKES 2 ROUND LOAVES

25g (1 oz) fresh yeast or
   15 g (½ oz) dried yeast plus
   ½ teaspoon sugar
375 ml (13 fl oz) warm water
350 g (12 oz) rye flour

350 g (12 oz) wholewheat flour
1 tablespoon salt
15 g (½ oz) butter
125 g (4 oz) black treacle
2 teaspoons cumin seeds

Dissolve yeast in the water; if using dried yeast add sugar too and leave 10-15 minutes to froth. Mix flours and salt, rub in butter, then add treacle, cumin and yeast liquid. Mix to a dough, knead 5-10 minutes. Place in a bowl, cover and leave until doubled in size: 1 hour in a warm place. Knock back, re-knead briefly. Form into two round loaves, place on greased baking sheets, cover and leave for 30 minutes, until well-risen. Set oven to 230°C (450°F), gas mark 8. Bake loaves for 10 minutes, then reduce setting to 200°C (400°F), gas mark 6 and bake for 25 minutes. Cool.

Swedish Tea Ring

A pretty semi-sweet yeast cake made in the form of a ring and decorated with icing, cherries and almonds.

SERVES 8-10

1 quantity of dough as given for
   poppy seed plait (page 51),
   kneaded and risen once
50 g (2 oz) melted butter

50 g (2 oz) soft brown sugar
1 teaspoon cinnamon
white glacé icing, glacé cherries
   and flaked almonds

Knock back dough, then roll dough to a rectangle 9 in x 12 in. Brush with melted butter, sprinkle with the sugar and cinnamon. Roll up like a swiss roll then form into a ring. Place on greased baking sheet and with scissors make slashes at an angle 2.5 cm (1 in) apart, and pull out the cut sections. Cover and leave in a warm place until puffy: about 30 minutes. Set oven to 190°C (375°F), gas mark 5. Bake ring for 30-35 minutes. Decorate with glacé cherries and nuts.

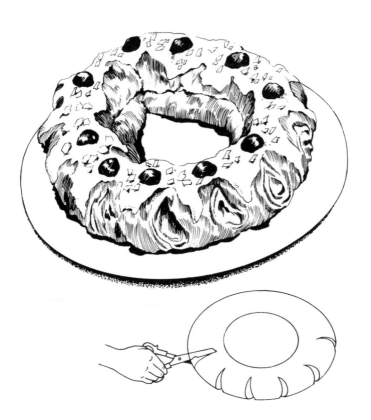

Savarin

A wonderfully impressive pudding that's easy to make.

SERVES 8-10

1 level tablespoon dried yeast
6 tablespoons lukewarm milk
150 g (5 oz) sugar
225 g (8 oz) flour
1 teaspoon salt
4 eggs

125 g (4 oz) soft butter
4 tablespoons each water and
    rum
4 tablespoons apricot jam, sieved
    and warmed

Put dried yeast, milk, 25 g (1 oz) sugar and 50 g (2 oz) of the flour into a bowl and mix. Cover, leave in warm place until sponge-like: 30-40 minutes. Then add the rest of the flour, salt, eggs and butter. Beat vigorously for 4-5 minutes. Pour into greased 20-22 cm (8-9 in) ring mould: it should half-fill it. Cover, leave 30-40 minutes until risen almost to top. Bake at 200°C (400°F), gas mark 6 for 20-25 minutes. Turn out on to wire rack, cool, then prick with skewer. Heat remaining sugar in water until dissolved; add rum, pour over cake, brush with apricot jam. Fill centre with fresh or poached fruit, decorate with whipped cream.

Wholewheat Stick

MAKES ONE LOAF

15 g (½ oz) fresh yeast or
   2 teaspoons dried yeast and
   ½ teaspoon sugar
300 ml (½ pint) warm water

450 g (1 lb) wholewheat flour
1 teaspoon salt
15 g (½ oz) butter or margarine
kibbled wheat

Blend yeast with water: if using dried yeast add ½ teaspoon sugar and leave 10-15 minutes to froth. Combine flour and salt in large bowl, rub in butter or margarine. Add yeast liquid, mix to a dough. Knead for 5-10 minutes, until smooth, then put dough into a bowl, cover and leave until doubled in bulk: 1 hour in a warm place. Knock back dough. Knead briefly, then roll dough into a long stick, sprinkle with kibbled wheat, place on a greased baking tray. Slash top of stick several times with a sharp knife, then cover with polythene and leave in a warm place for 30-45 minutes, until puffy. Set oven to 220°C (425°F), gas mark 7. Bake stick for 25-30 minutes, until it sounds hollow when tapped. Cool on a wire rack.

Wholewheat Tin Loaf

MAKES FIVE 450 G (1 LB) LOAVES

900 ml (32 fl oz) warm water
50 g (2 oz) fresh yeast or
    25 g (1 oz) dried yeast and
    ½ teaspoon sugar
1.5 kg (3 lb 5 oz) bag wholewheat
    flour

2 tablespoons sugar
4 teaspoons salt
50 g (2 oz) soft butter or
    margarine
kibbled wheat

Dissolve yeast in a cupful of the measured water: for dried yeast add ½ teaspoon sugar and leave 10-15 minutes until frothy. Combine flour, sugar and salt in a large bowl: rub in butter or margarine. Add yeast liquid and rest of water, mix to a dough. Knead for 10 minutes then put into a bowl, cover and leave until doubled in bulk: 1 hour in a warm place. Knock back, re-knead briefly. Divide into five equal pieces, shape, sprinkle with kibbled wheat and place in greased tins. Cover, put in a warm place until dough reaches tops of tins at sides and higher in centre. Bake at 230°C (450°F), gas mark 8 for 10 minutes then reduce to 200°C (400°F), gas mark 6 for 25 minutes. Cool loaves on wire rack.

Index